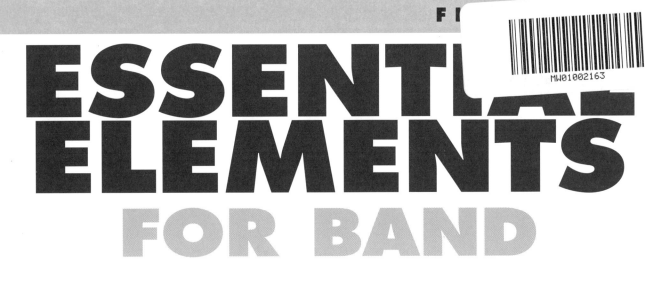

ESSENTIAL ELEMENTS FOR BAND

COMPREHENSIVE BAND METHOD

TIM LAUTZENHEISER

JOHN HIGGINS

CHARLES MENGHINI

PAUL LAVENDER

TOM C. RHODES

DON BIERSCHENK

To create an account, visit:
www.essentialelementsinteractive.com

Student Activation Code
E2FH-4141-2707-1440

ISBN 978-0-634-01295-2

HAL•LEONARD®
CORPORATION
7777 W. BLUEMOUND RD. P.O. BOX 13819 MILWAUKEE, WI 53213

REVIEW

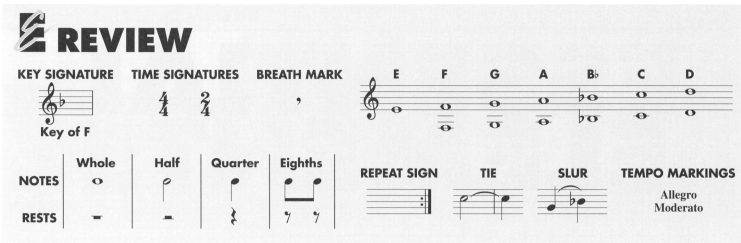

1. TECHNIQUE TRAX

2. SHOO FLY
American Folk Song

Allegro

3. THAILAND LULLABY
Thai Folk Song

Moderato

4. SHEPHERD'S HEY
English Folk Song

Moderato

5. THE CRAWDAD SONG
American Folk Song

Allegro

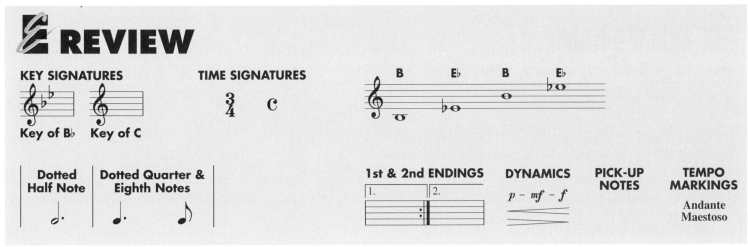

REVIEW

KEY SIGNATURES — Key of B♭, Key of C

TIME SIGNATURES — 3/4, C

Dotted Half Note, **Dotted Quarter & Eighth Notes**

1st & 2nd ENDINGS, **DYNAMICS** *p – mf – f*, **PICK-UP NOTES**, **TEMPO MARKINGS** Andante, Maestoso

6. AMERICA/GOD SAVE THE QUEEN
Andante — Based on a Traditional Anthem

7. WEARING OF THE GREEN
Moderato — Irish Folk Song

8. ROSES FROM THE SOUTH
Allegro — Johann Strauss, Jr.

9. CRUISIN' THROUGH THE PARK
Moderato

10. TRUMPET VOLUNTARY — Duet
Maestoso — Jeremiah Clarke

4

REVIEW

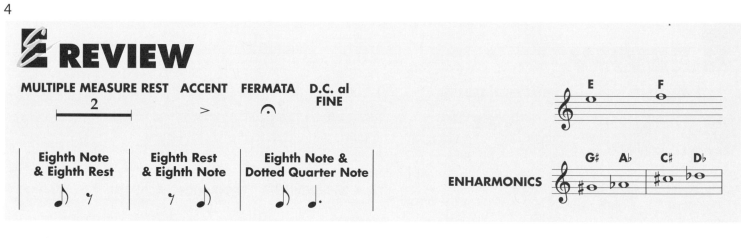

Staccato

Staccato notes are played lightly and with separation.
They are marked with a dot above or below the note.

15. TREADING LIGHTLY

Tenuto

Tenuto notes are played smoothly and connected, holding each note until the
next is played. They are marked with a straight line above or below the note.

16. SMOOTH MOVE

17. SHIFTING GEARS

English composer **Thomas Tallis** (1508–1585) served as a royal court composer for Kings Henry VIII and Edward VI, and Queens Mary and Elizabeth. During Tallis' lifetime, the artist Michaelangelo painted the Sistine Chapel.

Canons (one or more parts imitating the first part) were used in many forms by 16th century composers. A **Round** is a strict (or exact) canon which can be repeated any number of times without stopping. Play *Tallis Canon* as a 4-part round.

HISTORY

18. TALLIS CANON (Round)

Thomas Tallis

Sightreading

Sightreading means playing a musical piece for the first time. The key to sightreading success is to know what to look for *before* you play. Use the word **S-T-A-R-S** to remind yourself what to look for, and eventually your band will become sightreading STARS!

S — **Sharps or flats** in the key signature
T — **Time signature** and **tempo markings**
A — **Accidentals** not found in the key signature
R — **Rhythms**, silently counting the more difficult notes and rests
S — **Signs**, including dynamics, articulations, repeats and endings

19. SIGHTREADING CHALLENGE

DAILY WARM-UPS

WORK-OUTS FOR TONE & TECHNIQUE

20. TONE BUILDER

21. FLEXIBILITY STUDY

22. TECHNIQUE TRAX

23. CHORALE

Johann Sebastian Bach

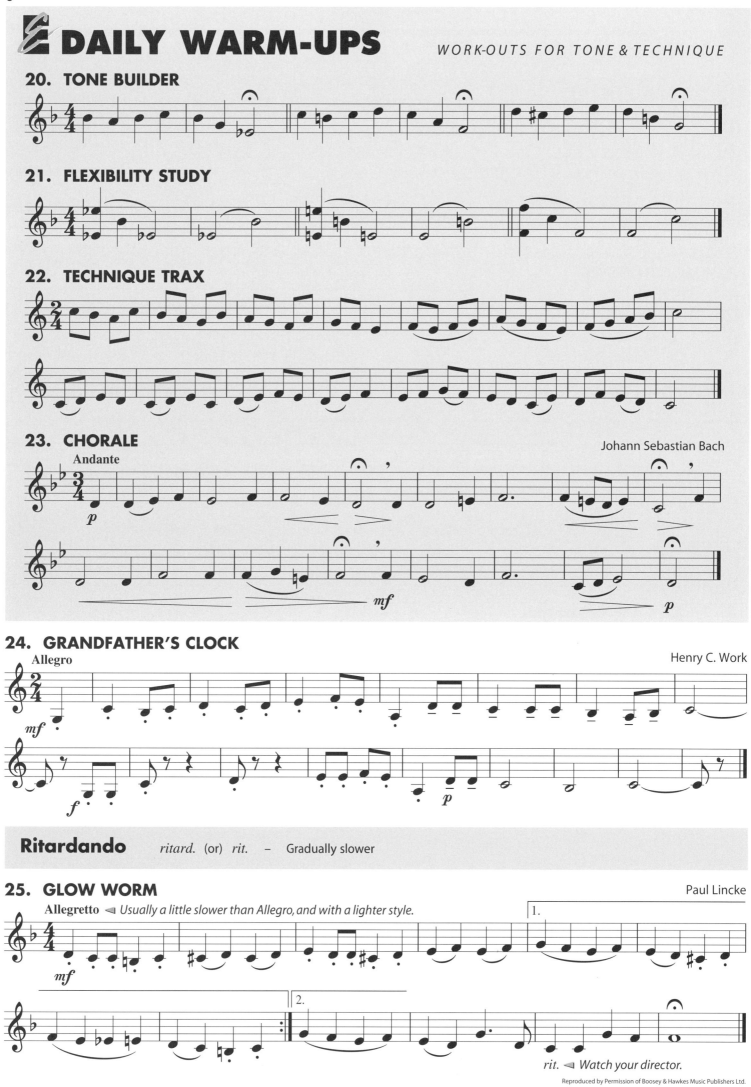

24. GRANDFATHER'S CLOCK

Henry C. Work

Ritardando

ritard. (or) *rit.* — Gradually slower

25. GLOW WORM

Paul Lincke

Allegretto ◁ *Usually a little slower than Allegro, and with a lighter style.*

rit. ◁ *Watch your director.*

26. ALMA MATER

A.C. Weekes, W.M. Smith, H.S. Thompson

The Scottish folk song *Loch Lomond* is credited to an anonymous soldier who was imprisoned and awaiting execution. In it he writes of his desire to return home to his family and the breathtaking beauty of Loch (Lake) Lomond, a lake in Scotland. Located in the southern highlands, the lake is almost entirely surrounded by hills. One of these is Ben Lomond, a peak 3,192 feet high.

HISTORY

27. LOCH LOMOND

Scottish Folk Song

Key Changes

If a key signature changes during a piece of music, you will usually see a thin double bar line at the **key change**. You may also see natural signs reminding you to "cancel" previous sharps or flats. Keep playing, using the correct notes indicated in the *new* key signature.

THEORY

28. MOLLY MALONE

Irish Folk Song

Dynamics

cresc. = crescendo (or)
decresc. = decrescendo (or)

29. RISE AND FALL

30. NO COMPARISON

31. SIGHTREADING CHALLENGE *Remember the S-T-A-R-S guidelines.*

8

THEORY

₵ Time Signature
Cut Time (Alla Breve)

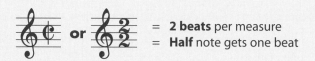 or = **2 beats** per measure
= **Half** note gets one beat

𝅝	= 2 beats
𝅗𝅥	= 1 beat
♩	= ½ beat

32. RHYTHM RAP *Clap the rhythm while counting and tapping.*

33. A CUT ABOVE

34. TWO-FOUR YANKEE DOODLE

American Folk Song

35. CUT TIME YANKEE DOODLE

American Folk Song

36. MARIANNE

Jamaican Folk Song

37. THE VICTORS

Louis Elbel

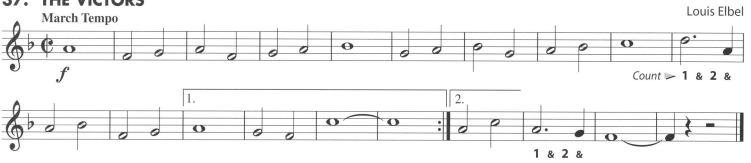

38. ESSENTIAL CREATIVITY *Write this example in cut time ₵ before playing.*

Dynamics

mp — *mezzo piano* (moderately soft)

Use full breath support at all dynamic levels.
p — *mp* — *mf* — *f*

39. A - ROVING

Syncopation

Syncopation occurs when an accent or emphasis is given to a note that is not on a strong beat. This type of "off-beat" feel is common in many popular and classical styles.

40. RHYTHM RAP

41. IN SYNC

42. LA ROCA

Puerto Rican Folk Song

American composer **George M. Cohan** (1878–1942) was also a popular author, producer, director and performer. He helped develop a popular form of American musical theater now known as musical comedy. He is also considered to be one of the most famous composers of American patriotic songs, earning the Congressional Medal of Honor in 1917 for his song *Over There*. Many of his songs became morale boosters when the United States entered World War I in that same year.

43. ESSENTIAL ELEMENTS QUIZ – YOU'RE A GRAND OLD FLAG

Words and Music by George M. Cohan

THEORY

New Key Signature

This key signature indicates your **Key of G** (Concert C).
Play all F's as F-sharp.

44. KEY MOMENT – New Note *Practice long tones on all new notes.*

45. THE MINSTREL BOY

Irish Folk Song

46. CLOSE CALL – New Note

47. VICTORY MARCH

M. J. Shea

THEORY

Cut Time Syncopation

Compare the notation of the melody below with *Victory March* above. Should they sound the same?

48. WINNING STREAK

M. J. Shea

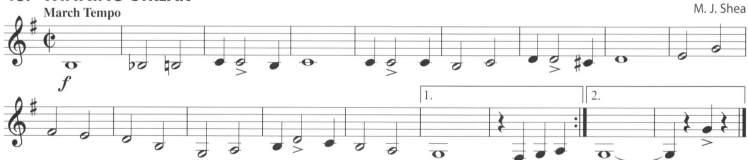

49. SIGHTREADING CHALLENGE *Remember the S-T-A-R-S guidelines.*

11

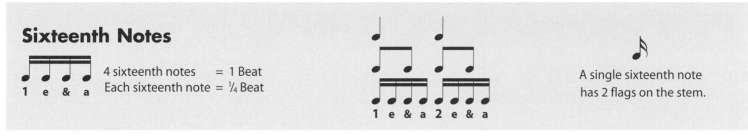

Sixteenth Notes

4 sixteenth notes = 1 Beat
Each sixteenth note = ¼ Beat

A single sixteenth note has 2 flags on the stem.

50. RHYTHM RAP

51. SIXTEENTH NOTE FANFARE

52. MOVING ALONG

53. BACK AND FORTH – Duet

54. COMIN' ROUND THE MOUNTAIN VARIATIONS

American Folk Song

55. ESSENTIAL ELEMENTS QUIZ

PERFORMANCE SPOTLIGHT

PERFORMANCE SPOTLIGHT

60. LAS MAÑANITAS – Band Arrangement

Mexican Folk Song
Arr. by John Higgins

61. RONDEAU – Band Arrangement

Jean-Joseph Mouret
Arr. by John Higgins

D.S. al Fine–Go back to the sign (𝄋) and play until **Fine**.

62. ROCK.COM – Encore Band Arrangement

John Higgins

THEORY

New Key Signature

This key signature indicates your **Key of F** (Concert Ab).
Play all B's as B-flat, all E's as E-flat, and all A's as A-flat.

Rallentando   *rall.* – Gradually slower (same as ritardando)

75. SIMPLE SONG – Duet

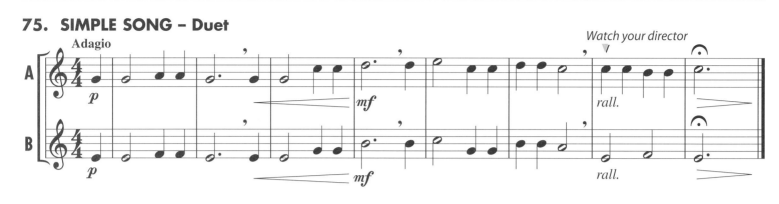

76. LINE DANCE

77. TECHNIQUE TRAX

78. THE GALWAY PIPER

Irish Reel

79. MANHATTAN BEACH MARCH

John Philip Sousa

80. SIGHTREADING CHALLENGE   *Remember the S-T-A-R-S guidelines.*

81. RHYTHM RAP

82. MARCHING ALONG

83. FANFARE FOR BAND – Trio

84. O TANNENBAUM

German Carol

85. S'VIVON

Traditional Hanukkah Song

86. GOOD KING WENCESLAS

English Carol

DAILY WARM-UPS

WORK-OUTS FOR TONE & TECHNIQUE

87. TONE BUILDER *Play at a very slow tempo.*

88. FLEXIBILITY STUDY

89. TECHNIQUE TRAX

90. CHORALE

Johann Sebastian Bach

HISTORY

French composer **Georges Bizet** (1838–1875) entered the Paris Conservatory to study music when he was only ten years old. There he won many awards for voice, piano, organ, and composition. Bizet's best known composition is the opera *Carmen,* which was first performed in 1875. *Carmen* tells the story of a band of Gypsies, soldiers, smugglers, and outlaws. Originally criticized for its realism on stage, it was soon hailed as the most popular French opera ever written.

91. TOREADOR SONG (from CARMEN)

Georges Bizet

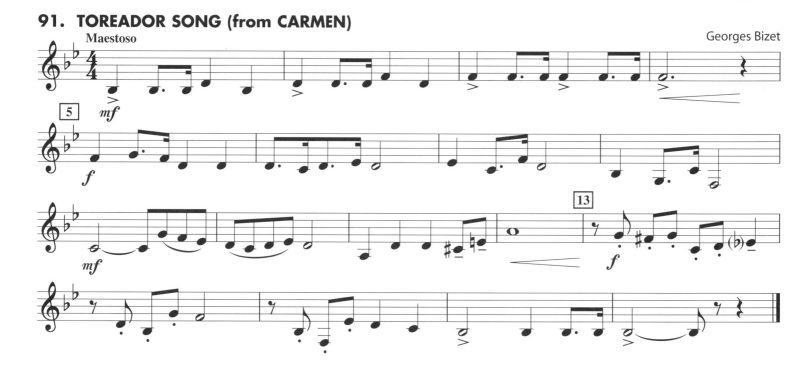

92. LA CUMPARSITA

G. Rodriguez

Moderato

Enharmonics

93. THE YELLOW ROSE OF TEXAS   *Check the key signature.*

American Folk Song

Moderato

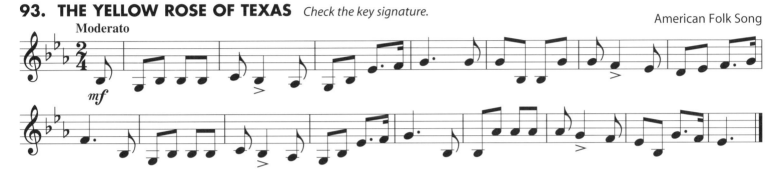

94. SCALE STUDY

Bb *Scale*

Check rhythm

Until 1974 Australia's official national anthem was *God Save The Queen.* A competition was held in 1973 to compose a new anthem, but none of the entries met with the judges' approval. Finally the government asked the public to vote, choosing from among Australia's 3 most popular patriotic songs. After easily defeating *Waltzing Matilda* and *God Save The Queen, Advance Australia Fair* was officially declared the national anthem of Australia on April 19, 1974.

HISTORY

95. ADVANCE AUSTRALIA FAIR

Peter Dodds McCormick

Maestoso

rit.   *a tempo*
▲ *Resume previous tempo*

96. ESSENTIAL CREATIVITY

Arrange the melody of "America (My Country 'Tis Of Thee)" for your instrument. Write out the first line (6 measures). Your first note is C. ADD: Key signature—key of C • Time signature—3/4 • Tempo and dynamic markings.

Play the completed line on your instrument to hear your own version.

97. AMERICAN PATROL

F. W. Meacham

Moderato

98. ARIA (from MARRIAGE OF FIGARO)

Wolfgang Amadeus Mozart

Moderato

HISTORY

American composer **John Philip Sousa** (1854–1932) was best known for his brilliant band marches. Sousa wrote 136 marches, including *The Stars and Stripes Forever,* which was declared the official march of the United States of America in 1987.

99. THE STARS AND STRIPES FOREVER

John Philip Sousa

March Tempo

Check rhythm

100. SIGHTREADING CHALLENGE *Remember the S-T-A-R-S guidelines.*

Moderato

$\frac{6}{8}$ Time Signature

 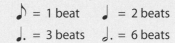

$\frac{6}{8}$ = **6 beats** per measure
= **Eighth** note gets one beat

♪ = 1 beat   ♩ = 2 beats
♩. = 3 beats   𝅗𝅥. = 6 beats

6/8 time is usually played with a slight emphasis on the **1st** and **4th** beats of each measure. This divides the measure into 2 groups of 3 beats each. In faster music, these two primary beats will make the music feel like it's counted "in 2."

101. RHYTHM RAP *Clap the rhythm while counting and tapping.*

102. LAZY DAY

103. ROW YOUR BOAT

104. JOLLY GOOD FELLOW

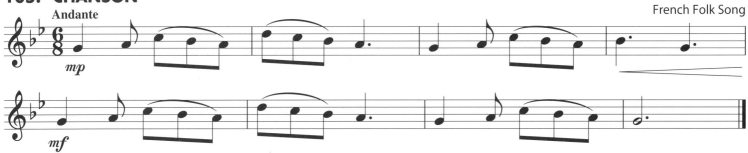

105. CHANSON

French Folk Song

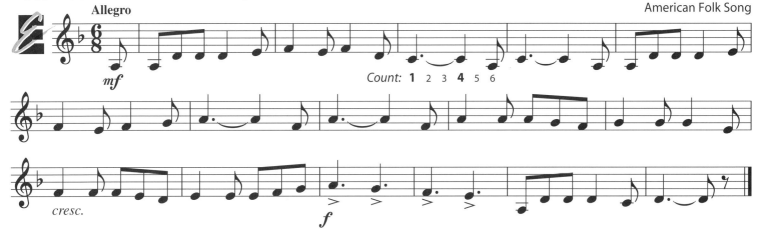

106. ESSENTIAL ELEMENTS QUIZ – WHEN JOHNNY COMES MARCHING HOME

American Folk Song

THEORY

More Enharmonics

Remember that notes which sound the same but have different letter names are called **enharmonics**. These are some common enharmonics that you'll use in the exercises below.

More Chromatics

The smallest distance between two notes is a half-step, and a scale made up of consecutive half-steps is a **chromatic scale**. These are usually written with **enharmonic** notes—sharps when going up and flats when going down.

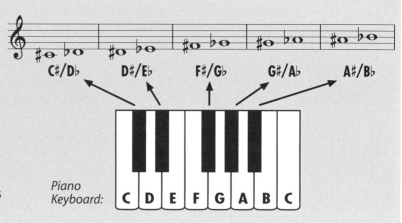

Piano Keyboard:

---

107. CHROMATIC SCALE *Practice slowly until you are sure of all the fingerings.*

108. TECHNIQUE TRAX

HISTORY

A **Habañera** is a Cuban dance and song form in slow 2/4 meter. It is named after the city of Havana, the capital of Cuba. Made popular in the New World in the early 19th Century, it was later carried over to Spain. There the rhythms of the Habañera were incorporated into many styles of Latin music. One of the most famous Habañeras is heard in Bizet's *Carmen,* written in 1875.

109. HABAÑERA (from CARMEN)

Georges Bizet

Andante ▽ F# *Enharmonic*

110. CHROMATIC CRESCENDO

Moderato

111. TURKISH MARCH (from THE RUINS OF ATHENS)
Ludwig van Beethoven

112. THE OVERLANDER
Australian Folk Song

113. STACCATO STUDY

Ab Enharmonic   F# Enharmonic

114. YANKEE DOODLE DANDY
Words and Music by George M. Cohan

115. SIGHTREADING CHALLENGE
Remember the **S-T-A-R-S** guidelines:
S – Sharps or flats in the key signature, **T** – Time signature and tempos, **A** – Accidentals, **R** – Rhythm, **S** – Signs

THEORY

Triplets

A **triplet** is a group of **3** notes played in the space of **2**. In 2/4, 3/4, or 4/4 time , an eighth note triplet is spread evenly across one beat.

116. RHYTHM RAP

117. THREE TO GET READY

118. TRIPLET STUDY

119. MARCH (from THE NUTCRACKER) – Duet

Peter I. Tchaikovsky

120. ESSENTIAL ELEMENTS QUIZ – THEME FROM FAUST

Charles Gounod

121. SCALE STUDY
C Scale

△ Check Rhythm

122. OVER THE RIVER AND THROUGH THE WOODS
American Folk Song

123. RHYTHM RAP

124. ON THE MOVE

125. HIGHER GROUND

126. ESSENTIAL ELEMENTS QUIZ

HISTORY

The first known printing of the lyrics and music to **The Marines' Hymn** dates from August 1, 1918. An unknown author is believed to have taken the opening words of the song from the words on the Marine Corps flag, "From the halls of Montezuma to the shores of Tripoli." The music was taken from "Genevieve de Brabant," by the operetta composer Jacques Offenbach.

127. THE MARINES' HYMN

D.S. al Fine

Play until you see the **D.S. al Fine**. Then go back to the sign (𝄋) and play until the word **Fine**. **D.S.** is the abbreviation for **Dal Segno**, or "from the sign," and **Fine** means "the end."

128. D.S. MARCH

Accelerando

accel. – Gradually faster.

129. CAN–CAN

Jacques Offenbach

130. TARANTELLA

Allegro

Italian Folk Song

f Pick-up   *mf*

The **waltz** is a dance in moderate 3/4 time which developed around 1800 from the Ländler, an Austrian peasant dance. Austrian composer **Johann Strauss, Jr.** (1825–1899) composed over 400 waltzes. These include such famous pieces as *The Blue Danube, Tales From the Vienna Woods* and *Emperor Waltz.*

131. EMPEROR WALTZ

Andantino ◁ *Tempo between Andante and Moderato.*

Johann Strauss, Jr.

mp   *f*   1.   2.   *rit.*   > >

Legato Style

legato – Played in a smooth, connected style.

132. ENGLISH DANCE – Duet

Johann Christian Bach

Andante

A   *mp legato*

B   *mp legato*   ▲ Smooth, connected

A   *mp*   *mf* rall.   *p*

B   *mp*   *mf* rall.   *p*

133. ESSENTIAL ELEMENTS QUIZ – BRITISH GRENADIERS

Traditional

Allegretto   1.   2.

mf   *mp*   *cresc.*   *f*

134. NASSAU BOUND

Bahamian Folk Song

Moderato

mf

1 & 2 & 3 & 4 &
△ *Count*

135. UNFINISHED SYMPHONY THEME

Franz Schubert

Andante

mp legato

136. RHYTHM STUDY

Measure Repeat   ./.   Repeat the previous measure once for each **Measure Repeat** sign.

137. COUNTRY GARDENS

English Folk Song

Allegretto

mf

f

△ *Measure Repeat*

mf

rall.

138. JOSHUA

African-American Spiritual

Allegro

mf ———— *f*

mf ———— *f*

139. LISTEN TO THE MOCKINGBIRD

Moderato

Alice Hawthorne

140. ANCHORS AWEIGH

March Tempo

Capt. A.H. Miles and C.A. Zimmerman

141. GREENSLEEVES

Andante

English Folk Song

142. THE LONG CLIMB

△ Measure Repeat

143. THE BLUE BELLS OF SCOTLAND

Moderato

Scottish Folk Song

Major and Minor

The scales you've already learned are called **Major** scales. They all follow the same pattern, with **half-steps** between notes 3–4 and between notes 7–8.

Natural Minor scales follow a different pattern, with **half-steps** between notes 2–3 and 5–6. The **D Minor** scale uses the same key signature as **F Major**.

Another type of minor scale is called **Harmonic Minor**, which adds an accidental to raise the **7th** note by a half-step. Compare the scales on the right.

See page 37 for additional minor scales.

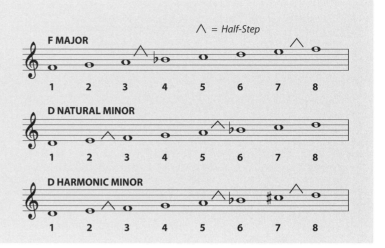

THEORY

144. NATURAL MINOR SCALE

145. FINALE FROM "NEW WORLD SYMPHONY"

Antonin Dvořák

146. HARMONIC MINOR SCALE

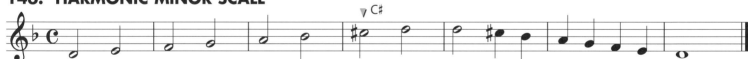

147. HUNGARIAN DANCE NO. 5

Johannes Brahms

148. POMP AND CIRCUMSTANCE (LAND OF HOPE AND GLORY)

Edward Elgar

PERFORMANCE SPOTLIGHT

D.S. al Coda — Play until you see the **D.S. al Coda**. Then go back to the sign (𝄋) and play until the **Coda Sign** ("To Coda" ⊕). Skip directly to the **Coda** and play until the end.

149. SIMPLE GIFTS – Band Arrangement

Shaker Folk Song
Arr. by John Higgins

150. SEMPER FIDELIS – Band Arrangement

John Philip Sousa
Arr. by John Higgins

PERFORMANCE SPOTLIGHT

151. DANNY BOY – Band Arrangement

Irish Folk Song
Arr. by John Higgins

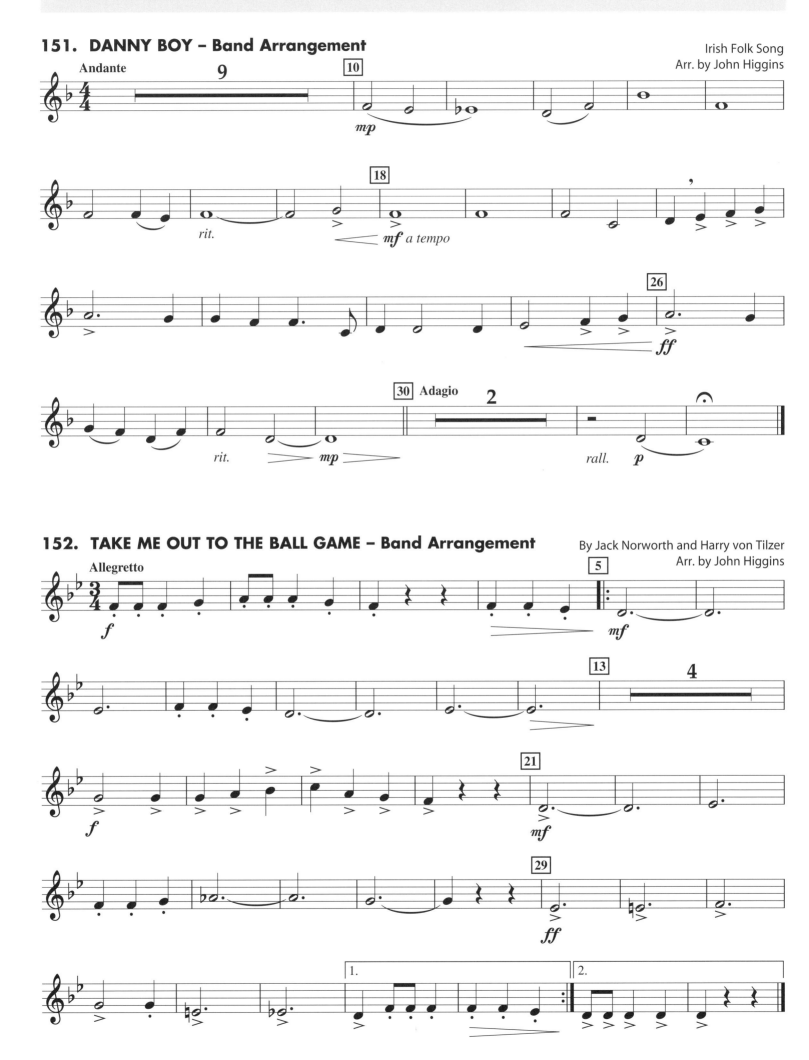

152. TAKE ME OUT TO THE BALL GAME – Band Arrangement

By Jack Norworth and Harry von Tilzer
Arr. by John Higgins

PERFORMANCE SPOTLIGHT

153. SERENGETI (AFRICAN RHAPSODY) – Band Arrangement

John Higgins

RUBANK® STUDIES

154. CHORALE (Concert B♭)

155. CHORALE (Concert E♭)

156. CHORALE (Concert F)

157. CHORALE (Concert A♭)

158. CHORALE (Concert C)

F HORN KEY OF F (CONCERT B♭)

159.

160.

161.

162.

RUBANK® STUDIES

F HORN KEY OF B♭ (CONCERT E♭)

163.

164.

165.

166.

F HORN KEY OF C (CONCERT F)

167.

168.

169.

170.

RUBANK® STUDIES

F HORN KEY OF E♭ (CONCERT A♭)

171.

172.

173.

174.

F HORN KEY OF G (CONCERT C)

175.

176.

177.

178.

RUBANK® STUDIES

F HORN KEY OF D MINOR (CONCERT G MINOR)

179.

180.

F HORN KEY OF G MINOR (CONCERT C MINOR)

181.

182.

F HORN KEY OF A MINOR (CONCERT D MINOR)

183.

184.

CHROMATIC SCALES

185.

186.

INDIVIDUAL STUDY – F Horn

187. TONE BUILDER *CD Track 56*

188. FLEXIBILITY STUDY *CD Track 57*

189. ARPEGGIO CHALLENGE *CD Track 58*

190. MELODY PATTERNS *CD Track 59*

191. ARTICULATION WORK-OUT *CD Track 60*

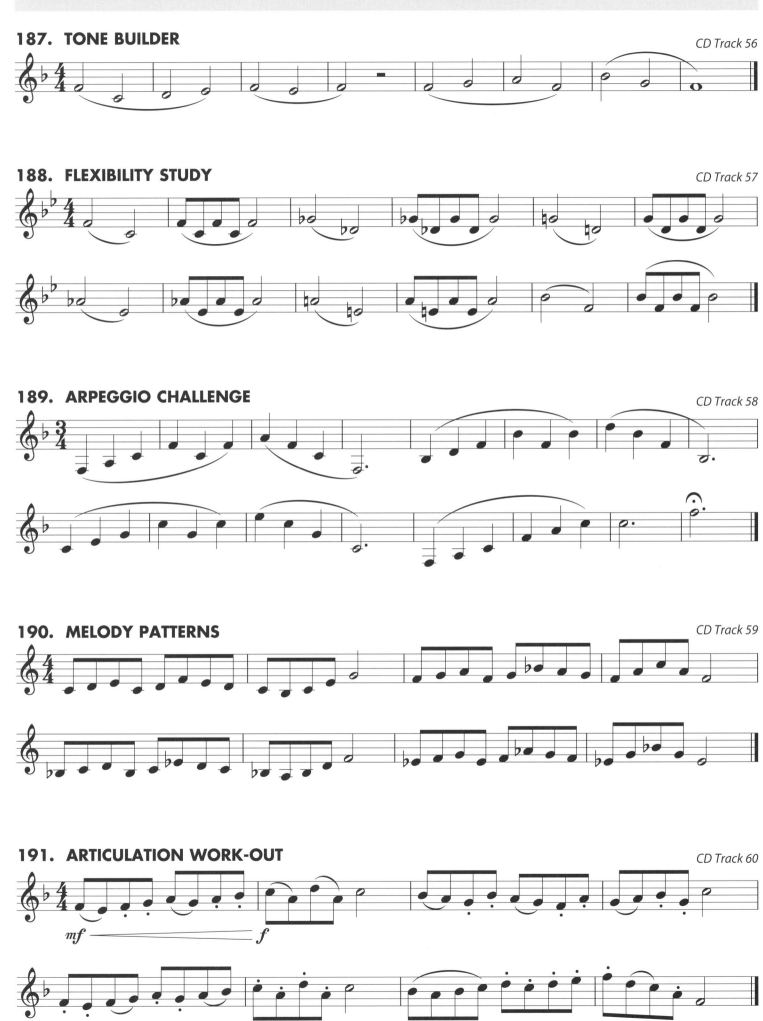

INDIVIDUAL STUDY – F Horn

192. TECHNIQUE STUDY
CD Track 61

193. CHROMATIC ETUDE
CD Track 62

194. LOW CHROMATIC STUDY
CD Track 63

195. SKILL BUILDER #1
CD Track 64

196. SKILL BUILDER #2
CD Track 65

INDIVIDUAL STUDY – F Horn

Solo with Piano Accompaniment

You can perform this solo with the piano accompaniment on the following page.

197. ROMANZE from "Concerto No. 3, KV 447 – F Horn Solo *CD Track 66*

Wolfgang Amadeus Mozart
Arr. by H. Voxman

INDIVIDUAL STUDY – F Horn

197. ROMANZE from "Concerto No. 3, KV 447" – Piano Accompaniment Wolfgang Amadeus Mozart
CD Track 67 Arr. by H. Voxman

RHYTHM STUDIES

RHYTHM STUDIES

CREATING MUSIC

Theme and Variation

Theme and Variation is a technique used by composers and arrangers to create interesting musical ideas that are "varied" from an established melody, or "theme." Play the following theme and two variations to hear how the arranger has created new phrases based on the original melody.

1. THEME

"Simple Gifts"

VARIATION 1 *Adding some notes • Changing some rhythms*

VARIATION 2 *Removing notes • Changing rhythms • Adding accents • Adding notes*

2. THEME AND YOUR VARIATION *Write your own variation of this theme.*
Use your instrument to hear and try different ideas.

Theme

"Oh, Susanna"

Your Variation

Blues Improvisation

Improvisation using a **Blues Scale** is an important part of jazz and popular music. Musicians use combinations of these notes and various rhythms to create their own spontaneous solos over a 12 measure progression of chords.

Blues Scale

3. LET'S JAM *Use the indicated notes from the Blues Scale to create your own solo to play with the accompaniment (Line B).*

You can mark your progress through the book on this page. Fill in the stars as instructed by your band director.

ESSENTIAL ELEMENTS

STAR ACHIEVER

NAME_____

1. Page 2–4, Review
2. Page 5, Sightreading Challenge, No. 19
3. Page 6, Daily Warm-Ups
4. Page 7, Sightreading Challenge, No. 31
5. Page 8, Essential Creativity, No. 38
6. Page 9, EE Quiz, No. 43
7. Page 10, Sightreading Challenge, No. 49
8. Page 11, EE Quiz, No. 55
9. Page 12–13, Performance Spotlight
10. Page 15, EE Quiz, No. 74
11. Page 16, Sightreading Challenge, No. 80
12. Page 18, Daily Warm-Ups
13. Page 19, Essential Creativity, No. 96
14. Page 20, Sightreading Challenge, No. 100

15. Page 21, EE Quiz, No. 106
16. Page 22, Chromatic Scale, No. 107
17. Page 23, Sightreading Challenge, No. 115
18. Page 24, EE Quiz, No. 120
19. Page 25, EE Quiz, No. 126
20. Page 27, EE Quiz, No. 133
21. Page 30, Natural Minor Scale, No. 144
22. Page 30, Harmonic Minor Scale, No. 146
23. Page 30, Pomp and Circumstance, No. 148
24. Page 31, Performance Spotlight
25. Page 32, Performance Spotlight
26. Page 33, Performance Spotlight
27. Page 38–39, Individual Study
28. Page 40, Performance Spotlight

MUSIC — AN ESSENTIAL ELEMENT OF LIFE

FINGERING CHART

Instrument Care Reminders

Before putting your instrument back in its case after playing, do the following:

- Use the water key to empty water from the instrument. Blow air through it. If your horn does not have a water key, invert the instrument. You may also remove the main tuning slide, invert the instrument and remove excess water.
- Wipe the instrument off with a clean soft cloth. Return the instrument to its case.
- Remove the mouthpiece. Once a week, wash the mouthpiece with warm tap water. Dry thoroughly.

Be sure to grease the slides regularly. Your director will recommend special slide grease and valve oil, and will help you apply them when necessary.

CAUTION: If a slide, a valve or your mouthpiece becomes stuck, ask for help from your band director or music dealer. Special tools should be used to prevent damage to your instrument.

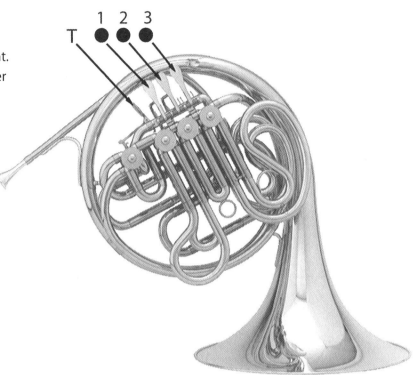

○ = Open
● = Pressed down
T = Trigger (Double Horn Only)

Instrument courtesy of Yamaha Corporation of America, Band and Orchestral Division

Using the Correct Fingering

Single Horn Players:
- F Horn players use the upper fingerings - marked "F Horn".
- B♭ Horn players use the lower fingerings - marked "B♭ Horn".
  *The trigger key (T) is only used on double horns.

Double Horn players:
- The trigger key (T) allows double horn players to switch between F and B♭ Horn.
- Use the "F Horn" fingering when the trigger key is **not** pressed.
  *For notes without a "T" fingering, the F Horn fingering is the recommended double horn fingering for that note.
- Use the "B♭ Horn" fingering when the trigger key is pressed.
  *For notes with a "T" fingering, the B♭ Horn fingering is the recommended double horn fingering for that note.

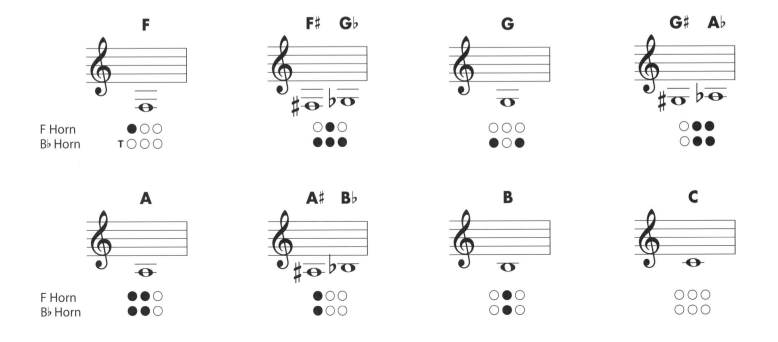

FINGERING CHART

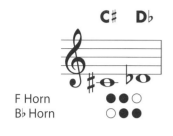

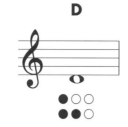

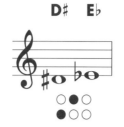

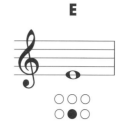

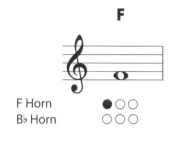

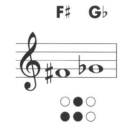

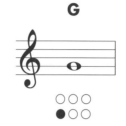

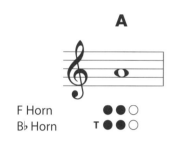

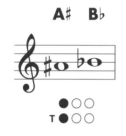

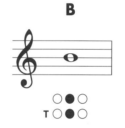

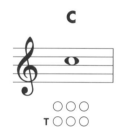

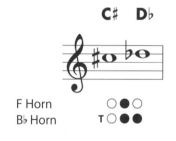

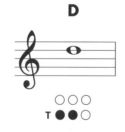

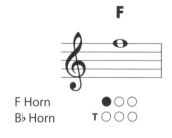

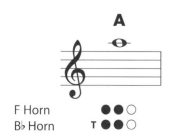

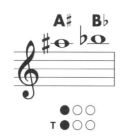

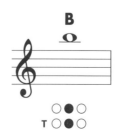

REFERENCE INDEX